AT THE PIANO WITH

MOZART

EDITED BY
MAURICE HINSON

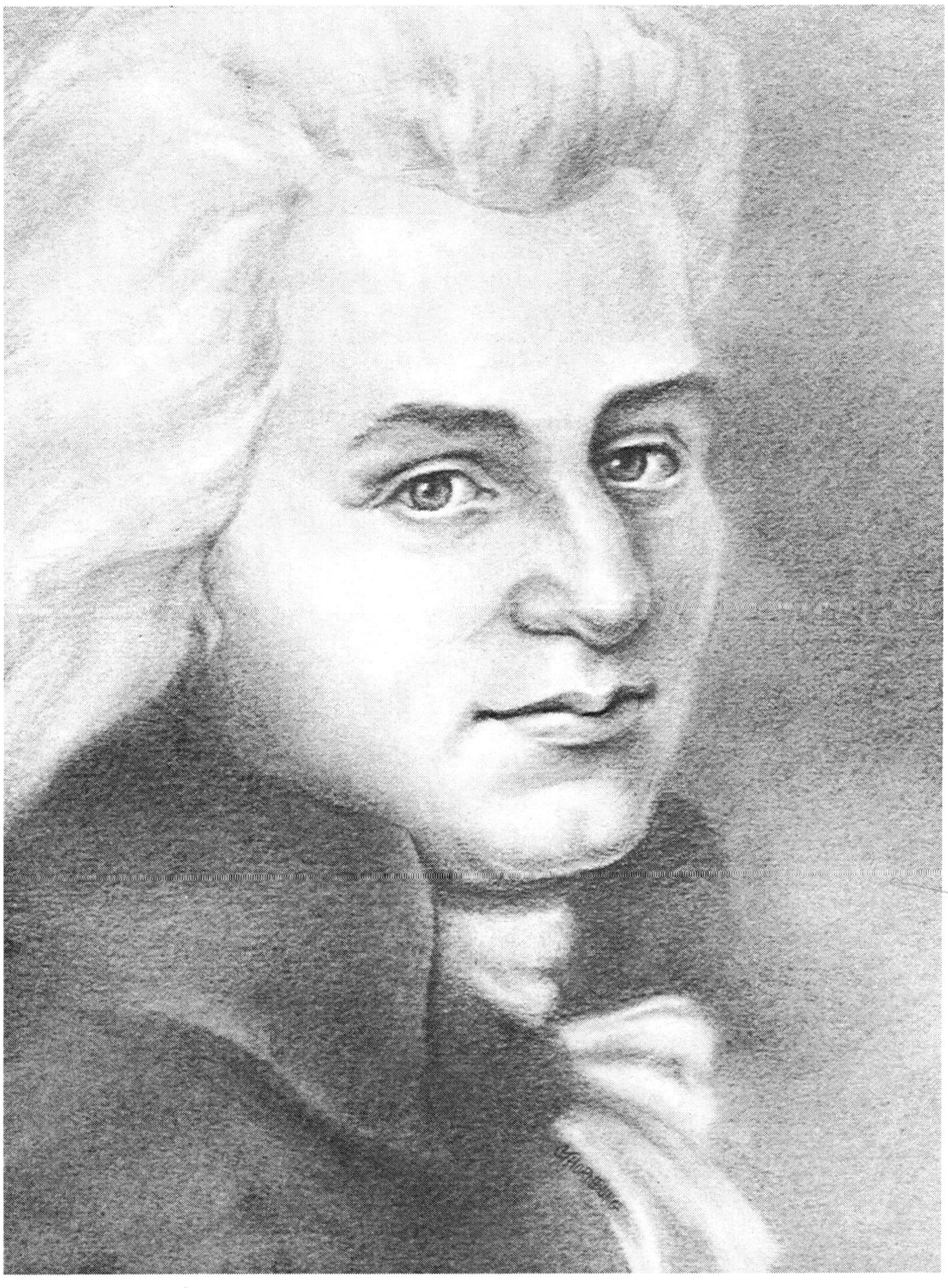

Illustration: Cheryl Thornburg
Cover Design: Ted Engelbart

This edition is dedicated to Lee Luvisi,
dear friend and colleague, and an inspiring Mozart performer.

To all Lovers of Sciences.

THE greateſt Prodigy that Europe, or that even Human Nature has to boaſt of, is, without Contradiction, the little German Boy WOLFGANG MOZART; a Boy, Eight Years old, who has, and indeed very juſtly, raiſed the Admiration not only of the greateſt Men, but alſo of the greateſt Muſicians in Europe. It is hard to ſay, whether his Execution upon the Harpſichord and his playing and ſinging at Sight, or his own Caprice, Fancy, and Compoſitions for all Inſtruments, are moſt aſtoniſhing. The Father of this Miracle, being obliged by Deſire of ſeveral Ladies and Gentlemen to poſtpone, for a very ſhort Time, his Departure from England, will give an Opportunity to hear this little Compoſer and his Siſter, whoſe muſical Knowledge wants not Apology. Performs every Day in the Week, from Twelve to Three o'Clock in the Great Room, at the Swan and Hoop, Cornhill. Admittance 2s. 6d. each Perſon.

The two Children will play alſo together with four Hands upon the ſame Harpſichord, and put upon it a Handkerchief, without ſeeing the Keys.

(*top*) Mozart in court costume, age six. Painting by Lorenzoni; (*above*) advertisement from the *Publick Advertizer*, London, June 1765.

CONTENTS

PAGE

FOREWORD

To Wolfgang Amadeus Mozart (1756–1791), music must have been as normal and as instinctively natural as breathing, and the easiness and perfection of his composing places his works above human frailty, above earthly laboriousness, and makes them something that one can only call superhuman, or... simply: nature's beauty transcribed in sound.

The simple, natural beauty of Mozart's music which covers, in spite of this apparent simplicity (which is really the masterful economy of a true genius) such a wide range of emotion and expression, should be recreated in the simplest, most natural way, with no other aim or incentive than the feeling of admiration and—perhaps—happiness that comes from playing this wonderful music.

This may sound paradoxical, but I feel that Mozart's piano music is described best by saying that it is at the same time the most easy and the most difficult music to play correctly.

In one way, it requires practically no particular effort; it is completely natural and easy to play Mozart; in another way, it might be called very difficult for a musician to attain the level where technical command, musical feelings and all the mental and psychic faculties are so harmoniously coordinated, that the fingers obey with the necessary amount of security the impulses of expression suggested by the natural flow and enchanting beauty of Mozart's melodic lines.

When I say "no particular effort," this means that the complete concentration on the task of performing a composition is taken for granted, and that the utmost attention is given to every detail of technique, musical value and mood of expression, at every moment and without interruption. But not every composer makes it so easy to proceed from this concentration to the state of communion, or identity between composer and performer.

Mozart is technically no problem to sensitive fingers, to fingers that are used to translating into sound the impulses given by the inner ear—or by fingers which know how to sing and breathe naturally in connection with the piano keys.

The Mozart Family, (*l. to r.*) Nannerl, Wolfgang and Leopold. (della Croce, *Mozart Museum, Salzburg.*)

MOZART AND THE CLAVIER

Clavier is a convenient term to cover the three keyboard instruments used by Mozart at different stages of his career—the clavichord, harpsichord, and fortepiano. For which of these did he write his many works for solo keyboard, for chamber music or concertos? This is a complicated question to which, as a whole, there is no absolutely definitive answer. It appears that Mozart did not compose specifically for the clavichord, and that his keyboard works composed before 1782 were, with a few possible exceptions, for the harpsichord, while those after that date were for the fortepiano. All three instruments were available in the Mozart household, and he went on playing the clavichord in private even up to 1789. But nothing suggests that he continued to play the harpsichord once the fortepiano had become generally available, for the fortepiano suited perfectly the needs of his rapidly evolving style of playing and composing.

18th century fortepiano by A. Stein. Upright pedal-piano has been built on. (*Metropolitan Museum, New York.*)

In Salzburg, the fortepiano was slow to be introduced, but on his travels Mozart had already played on a Stein fortepiano in Mannheim, Germany, as early as 1777. Here is part of his enthusiastic account of that experience written in a letter to his father on October 17 of that year:

> This time I shall begin at once with Stein's fortepianos. Before I had seen any of his make, Spath's claviers had always been my favourites. But now I much prefer Stein's for they damp ever so much better than the Regensburg instruments. When I strike hard, I can keep my finger on the note or raise it, but the sound ceases the moment I have produced it. In whatever way I touch the keys, the tone is always even. It never jars, it is never stronger or weaker or entirely absent; in a word, it is always even... His instruments have this special advantage over others that they are made with escape action. Only one maker in a hundred bothers about this. But without an escapement it is impossible to avoid jangling and vibration after the note is struck. When you touch the keys, the hammers fall back again the moment after they have struck the strings, whether you hold down the keys or release them.

The fortepiano had a graceful winglike shape, with a compass of five or five-and-a-half octaves, and was about seven feet long. The action was very light, and the force needed to depress the keys was only about one quarter of what is required on our modern grand piano. The strings were mostly of thin steel wire, those of the bass often of brass, being barely half as thick as those in the top octave of the modern grand piano. The hammers were covered with thin leather, and their swift contact and rebound from the strings produced a clear, singing tone, sonorous and vibrant in the bass and silvery in the middle and upper octaves. The natural quality of the sound was enhanced by the whole instrument being constructed of wood. Apart from Andreas Stein, the maker liked best by Mozart was Anton Walter of Vienna, one of whose instruments he acquired sometime between 1782 and 1784. It is now preserved and used in the Mozarteum in Salzburg.

From 1785 onwards Mozart used a pedal-board to reinforce the volume of his instrument, both for concert and teaching purposes. On March 12, 1785, Mozart's father Leopold wrote to his daughter: "He has had a large fortepiano pedal made, which is under the instrument and is about two feet longer and extremely heavy. It is taken to the Mehlgrube every Friday and has also been taken to Count Zichy's and to Prince Kaunitz's." In 1790, the pedal-board was noted by Joseph Frank, when he was taking lessons from Mozart. This pedal attachment had many uses. It could be used for increasing volume, by simply doubling the lower or middle notes of any passage, and it could serve to add harmonic richness, tonal variety, antiphonal or contrapuntal effects. With this aid the fortepiano could be used for practicing organ works with a pedal part, just as the pedal clavichord has been for generations. Surely Mozart used his skill as an organist to obtain the best possible effects from his massive pedal-board.

MOZART AS PERFORMER

There were four instruments on which Mozart distinguished himself as a performer. During his younger years, his competence as a violinist won commendation from his father and from other contemporaries. But in 1781, after finally leaving his hometown of Salzburg, Austria, he gave up the violin almost entirely in favor of the viola which he played only in chamber music. His reputation on the organ was widespread throughout Europe, and he never lost an opportunity to play on famous or unfamiliar instruments wherever he traveled. In fact, Mozart was as well known throughout Europe as a virtuoso as he was as a composer. In continuous and decisive influence, it was the clavier which completely dominated his whole career. He continued as a virtuoso to his death in 1791.

Mozart in concert with his father Leopold and sister Nannerl. Paris, 1763.

It is possible to gain some idea of Mozart's style as a player from his own words. First, there is his statement that "above all things a player should possess a quiet, steady hand, the natural lightness, smoothness and gliding rapidity of which is so developed that the passages flow like oil."

The mechanism of the Stein fortepiano encouraged lightness, since the key-bedding was shallow, and consequently the best effect could be achieved by a hand that kept close to the keyboard. Mozart regarded accuracy and precision highly, with every detail clearly presented, and his *forte* was evidently not in the nature of a violent contrast. The smoothness "like oil" that he insisted upon so much, resulted from equality of touch on the Stein fortepiano, although it must have been acquired and equally in evidence on the harpsichord.

Mozart was particular in the position of the hand: it had to fall naturally and gently on the keyboard, much as though it had been fashioned for the purpose, and Clementi's bravura passages upset him because he thought they tended to disturb an essential balance and serenity and thus shocked the eye as well as the ear. Ease and repose at the keyboard would seem desirable for full artistic expression. This quiet hand, connected so closely to the shallow "Viennese action," was conducive to a fastidious clarity of detail and correctness of execution which enabled him to be sure that his passage work, to use his own simile, "flowed like oil." The simile is perhaps more uilitarian that the description of Chopin's velvety touch, or the "pearling" scales of Liszt, but it means the same thing.

There can be no doubt that the taste and feeling on which Mozart laid such stress existed in his own playing. He had his own views on *rubato* and must have depended on it to a large degree for his clarity of expression, but he teaches an important lesson to those pianists whose idea of expression is to rob music of its rhythm. The subtle implications of a free and independent right hand against a rigid and unbending left mean an equality that must be instinctive rather than manufactured. His staccato, in particular, seems to have impressed everyone by its gracious brilliance and "peculiar charm." Haydn said: "I will never forget his clavier-playing as long as I live; it went directly to the heart."

In tracing Mozart's artistic lineage as a keyboard performer, the question of formation of style is very important. His first teacher was his father, Leopold, a sound musician who is known as the author of a very fine violin method *Versuch einer gründlichen Violinschule*, written in 1756, and who continued as Mozart's adviser and critic to the end of his life in 1787. But Mozart's artistic education really began in the wider sense when he met Johann Christian Bach in London and came, through him, under Italian influences. It was there he composed his first symphonies, and the *London Notebook*, at the age of eight. ***At the Piano with Mozart*** contains a number of pieces from the *London Notebook*. J. C. Bach's influence is apparent in the clavier works of that period.

What Mozart did with this "period" idiom was to endow it with artistic beliefs and convictions and to use it supremely well. After a certain time his melody took on a more individual character but was still grounded in the period's general musical vocabulary.

We should remember that Mozart was a virtuoso, a master-pianist, in the best sense of the term. If he astounded his audiences with display, it was always in perfect accord with feeling and expression. Everything seems to support the fact that his main interest in life was music: in fact, it could be said that music was life itself to him. To Wolfgang, music was play, a joyful creative function, and this was the basis of his approach for the greater part of his life.

Mozart's letters contain a number of passages giving valuable information about the keyboard playing of others, and largely by inference, about his own style of playing. A description of the playing of Nanette Stein, a child prodigy of Augsburg, Germany, deserves quoting from a letter of October 23, 1777:

> Anyone who sees and hears her play and can keep from laughing, must, like her father, be made of stone. [*Stein* is the German word for stone. Mozart must have enjoyed this pun!] For instead of sitting in the middle of the clavier, she sits right up opposite the treble, as it gives her more chance of flopping about and making grimaces. She rolls her eyes and smirks. When a passage is repeated, she plays it more slowly the second time. If it has to be played a third time, the arm must be raised as high as possible, and according as the notes in the passage are stressed, the arm, not the fingers, must do this, and that too with great emphasis in a heavy and clumsy manner. But the best joke of all is that when she comes to a passage which ought to flow like oil and which necessitates a change of finger, she does not bother her head about it, but when the moment arrives, she just leaves out the notes, raises her hand and starts off again quite comfortably—a method by which she is much more likely to strike a wrong note, which often produces a curious effect. I am simply writing this in order to give Papa some idea of clavier-playing and clavier-teaching, so that he may derive some profit from it later on. Herr Stein is quite crazy about his daughter, who is eight and a half and who now learns everything by heart. She may succeed, for she has great talent for music. But she will not make progress by this method—for she will never acquire great rapidity, since she definitely does all she can to make her hands heavy. Further, she will never acquire the most essential, the most difficult and the chief requisite in music, which is time, because from her earliest years she has done her utmost not to play in time. . . He [Herr Stein] used to be quite crazy about Beecke; but now he sees and hears that I am the better player, that I do not make grimaces, and yet play with such expression, that, as he himself confesses, no one up to the present has been able to get such good results out of his fortepianos. Everyone is amazed that I can always keep strict time. What these people cannot grasp is that in tempo rubato in an Adagio, the left hand should go on playing in strict time.

We learn from this letter that Mozart sat quietly at the middle of the keyboard and played without making faces. We learn that he did not change tempo in repeated sections of a piece, although he probably varied it by adding ornaments, etc. We also learn that he did not like the arm to be raised and that he favored a light wrist with the fingers always in contact with the keys. And one of the most important things we learn relates to his use of *tempo rubato*: the left hand provides an accompaniment in strict time while the right hand plays an independent *espressivo*, carrying the melody somewhat like a singer—much easier to describe than to perform!

In 1778, Mozart had some very severe words concerning his famous contemporary Abbé Vogler's (George Joseph Vogler, 1749-1814) playing in a letter dated January 17:

> He took the first movement prestissimo—the Andante allegro and the Rondo even more prestissimo. He generally played the bass differently from the way it was written, inventing now and then quite another harmony and melody. Nothing else is possible at that pace, for the eyes cannot see the music nor the hands perform it . . .
>
> The listeners (I mean those who deserve the name) can only say that they have seen music and piano-playing. They hear, think and—feel as little during the performance as the player himself. Well, you may easily imagine that it was unendurable. At the same time, I could not bring myself to say to him, *Far too quick!* Besides, it is much easier to play a thing quickly than slowly: in difficult passages you can leave out a few notes without anyone noticing it. But is that beautiful music? In rapid playing the right and left hands can be changed without anyone seeing or hearing it; but is that beautiful? And wherein consists of the art of playing *prima vista* [by sight]? In this: in playing the piece in the time in which it ought to be played and in playing all the notes, appoggiaturas and so forth, exactly as they are written and with the appropriate expression and taste, so that you might suppose that the performer had composed it himself. Vogler's fingering too is wretched; his left thumb is just like that of the late Adlgasser [Anton Adlgasser (1729-1777), Salzburg composer and clavierist; Mozart succeeded him as court organist] and he does all the treble runs with the thumb and first finger of his right hand.

Vogler obviously used the old pre-C. P. E. Bach style of fingering. Mozart probably never used it.

Another contemporary of whom Mozart notoriously disapproved on technical grounds was Muzio Clementi. On January 12, 1782, he wrote: "Clementi plays well, so far as execution with the right hand goes. His greatest strength lies in his passages in thirds. Apart from this, he has not a kreutzer's [penny's] worth of taste or feeling."

About G. F. Richter, a successful contemporary, Mozart expressed himself this way on April 28, 1784: "He plays well so far as execution goes, but, as you will discover when you hear him, he is too rough and labored and entirely devoid of taste and feeling."

From these criticisms, we are able to form some idea of the theoretical basis of Mozart's own approach to the keyboard. They also show something of his mental limitations, especially in regard to Clementi, whose advances in technique he failed to appreciate. Mozart did not realize how different the touch was of the shallow-bedded keys of the "Viennese" action compared with the deeper, less responsive touch of the English fortepiano to which Clementi was accustomed. Still, our exact knowledge of Mozart's playing is scanty. Accounts given by contemporaries are rather vague, and perhaps err on the side of adulation. But it does seem that though he may have been surpassed in technique by some of his contemporaries, such as Kozeluch and Sterkel, in depth, feeling, and imaginative power, he stood alone. There was, moreover, one aspect of Mozart's playing that earned him special renown, his prodigious improvisation. When his imagination was excited, he and his instrument were as one. One of the most eloquent of many testimonies is to be found in Schichtegroll's *Nekrolog* of 1793: "His whole countenance would change, his eyes became calm and collected; emotions spoke from every movement of his muscles, and was communicated by a sort of intuitive sympathy to his audience."

To this should be added the following more factual and highly illuminating description preserved by Vincent Novello (1781-1861). It is found in a passage of his diary which mentions his meeting with Viennese composers in 1829:

> He [Abbé Stadler] communicated to me the following curious anecdote, in my enquiring what were the most favourite pieces with Mozart when he was in private among his intimate friends. The Abbé said that he usually played *extemporaneously*, but that his imagination was so inexhaustible and at the same time his ideas were so symmetrical and regularly treated that Albrechtsberger could not be persuaded but that they were regular pieces that he had studied beforehand. One evening when Mozart, the Abbé Stadler and

Albrechtsberger were together, the latter asked Mozart to sit down to the instrument and play something. Mozart directly complied, but instead of taking a subject of his own he told Albrechtsberger to give him a theme. Albrechtsberger accordingly invented a subject on the spot and which he was quite certain that Mozart could not possibly have ever heard before; he also selected the most trivial features he could think of in order to put Mozart's ingenuity, invention, and creative power to the severest test.

This extraordinary genius immediately took the theme that had been given him thus unexpectedly and played for upwards of an hour upon it, treating it in all possible variety of forms of fugue, canon, from the most simple to the most elaborate counterpoint, until Albrechtsberger could hold no longer, but exclaimed in transport: "I am now perfectly convinced that your extemporaneous playing is really the thought of the moment, and that you fully deserve all the fame you have acquired for this wonderful talent."

It is most interesting to compare these passages with the following sentences taken from a description of him as a child of ten: "He was sometimes involuntarily attracted to his harpsichord as by a secret force, and drew from it sounds which were the lively expression of the idea with which he had just been occupied. One might say that at these moments he is himself the instrument in the hands of music and one may imagine him as composed of strings harmoniously put together with such skill that it is impossible to touch one without all the others being also set in motion."

An idea of his improvisation may be obtained from his published fantasies and variations, many of which undoubtedly started life as improvisations. The *Fantasy in D Minor*, K. 397 (385g), page 40, is probably a written-out improvisation as its style is much more pianistic than almost anything in the keyboard concertos and sonatas (see page 17 for information on "K" numbers). This leads to the supposition that while playing his own music, Mozart would have used a much more lavish and virtuoso-like technique than indicated by the printed notes that have come down to us. Therefore, it is vitally important for the interpreter of this music to realize that the spirit of improvisation must come into play even in the interpretation of pieces that have been precisely notated.

Anyone as sociable as Mozart was bound to be in continual demand at informal and semi-private gatherings to provide entertainment at the keyboard. Of the many accounts of his feats, one of the less familiar deserves quotation. It is taken from Michael Kelly, who sang in the first performance of "The Marriage of Figaro":

> He favoured the company by performing fantasias and capriccios on the fortepiano. His feeling, the rapidity of his fingers, the great execution and strength of his left hand particularly, and the apparent inspiration of his modulations, astounded me . . . He was kind-hearted, and always ready to oblige; but so very particular, when he played, that if the slightest noise was made, he instantly left off.

Another social form of music to which Mozart was partial was the playing of four-hand duets. Here is a quote from Kelly about the sister of his good friend, Padre Martini:

> When I was admitted to her conversations and musical parties, she was in the vale of years, yet still possessed the gaiety and vivacity of a girl, and was polite and affable to all. Mozart was an almost constant attendant at her parties, and I have heard him play duets on the fortepiano with her, of his own composition. She was a great favourite of his.

Mozart also regularly performed duets with his sister, Maria Anna, called Nannerl by the family, his partner from the time of their early travels together until much later. A correspondent of Charles Burney's heard them play in Salzburg (prior to 1773), and we know that their partnership lasted until they were both adults.

All of this supports the idea that Mozart's playing brought his music to life by various means—by singing tone, by rhythmic verve, by tasteful phrasing, including clear differentiation between legato and detached notes, by dynamic nuance, by vital tempos, by rubato in slow movements, and, in their highest form, by all the indefinable elements that we include in the word "musicianship."

MOZART AS TEACHER

Mozart must have found it depressing that very few pupils approached his own standards either in virtuosity or powers of expression. "You happy man," he once remarked to Gyrowetz, who was about to start on a journey to Italy. "As for me, I am off now to give a lesson to earn my bread." While his attitude fluctuated in regard to the whole matter of keyboard performance and to having to devote so much time and energy to teaching, he seems ultimately to have accepted it as a necessary part of his life and as one which was not without its compensations. "Unless you wear yourself out," he wrote to his father from Paris on July 31, 1778, "by taking a large number of pupils, you cannot make much money." That some of his students were extremely slow must be inferred from several remarks in his letters, and we can only guess at the drudgery involved, of which there is a hint on a single sheet in Mozart's autograph (in the Fitzwilliam Museum, Cambridge), containing some quickly jotted-down five-finger exercises.

But he could take pains with a backward pupil and a good one caused him much pride. On June 9, 1784, he wrote to his father: "I am fetching Paisiello in my carriage, as I want him to hear both my pupil and my compositions." This pupil was Barbara Ployer, for whom he had composed his Concertos in E flat (K. 449) and G (K. 453). Another girl in whose playing he delighted was Franziska von Jacquim, of whom he wrote on January 14, 1787: "I have never yet had a pupil who was so diligent and who showed so much zeal—and indeed I am looking forward to giving her lessons again according to my small ability." We get a hint of the bond between himself and some of his students when we read in his father's letter of November 19, 1784, that to celebrate his name-day, he "gave a small musical party, at which his pupils performed."

Mozart's account of his teaching Rosa Cannabich at Mannheim contains the following interesting passages taken from letters of November 14–16, 1777:

> The Andante [of the sonata K. 309] will give us most trouble, for it is full of expression and must be played accurately and with the exact shades of forte and piano, precisely as they are marked. She is very smart and learns very easily. Her right hand is very good, but her left, unfortunately, is completely ruined. I can honestly say that I often feel quite sorry for her when I see her struggling, as she so often does, until she really gets quite out of breath, not from lack of skill but simply because she cannot help it, for she has got into the habit of doing what she does, as no one has ever shown her any other way. I have told her mother and I have told her too that if I were her regular teacher, I would lock up all her music, cover the keys with a handkerchief and make her practise, first with the right hand and then with the left, nothing but passages, trills, mordants and so forth, very slowly at first, until each hand should be thoroughly trained. I would then undertake to turn her into a first-rate clavierist.

It appears that Mozart was not an ideal teacher, due to certain flaws in his character. He never suffered fool's flattery and in his earlier years, during the time of his stay in Paris, was too lazy to involve himself with teaching. Later, despite his spasmodic and harassed way of life, he made an effort to keep to a routine, although his irregular concert engagements and travel must have made it difficult to meet students on a regular basis. In February, 1782, he normally taught from nine to one. Exactly two years later he wrote to his father on February 10: "I spend the whole morning giving lessons, so I have only the evening to spare for my beloved task—composition."

Mozart's financial situation was so desperate by May, 1790, that he wrote to his generous friend, Puchberg, on the 17th: "I now have two pupils and should very much like to raise the number to eight. Do your best to spread the news that I am willing to give lessons." We do not know what Mozart's fees were, nor whether he charged his aristocratic pupils at a different rate from his other pupils. Nor have we definite evidence as to the length of time of his lessons. But it is almost certain that he had many more pupils than those whose names, barely a dozen in all, have been preserved.

There is nothing to show that musicians such as Attwood, Eberl, and Süssmayr, who were Mozart's pupils in theory and composition, also took lessons in playing the fortepiano. While probable, I cannot prove that Anton Liste (1774-1832) may have done both from 1789 onward. Among non-musicians, there was Joseph Frank, a Viennese doctor who received 12 lessons in 1790. His account runs:

> I found Mozart a little man with a large head and plump hands, and was somewhat coldly received by him. "Now," said he, "play me something." I played a Fantasia of his own composition. "Not bad," said he, to my great astonishment, "but now listen to me play it." It was a miracle! The clavier became another instrument under his hands. It was strengthened by a second clavier which served him as a pedal. Mozart then made some remarks as to the way in which I should perform the Fantasia. I was fortunate enough to understand him. "Do you play any other of my compositions?" "Yes," I answered, "your Variations on the theme "Unser dummer Pobel meint" [K. 455], and a Sonata with accompaniments for violin and violoncello." "Good, I will play you that piece; you will profit more by hearing me than playing them yourself."

We have a glimpse of Mozart's attitude towards teaching tempo in certain types of works. Sending his sister a piece, possibly the *Capriccio in C*, K. 395, he wrote: "You need not be very particular about the tempo. This is a peculiar kind of piece. It's the kind of thing that may be played as you feel inclined."

Title page to Mozart's first published work, "*Sonates pour le Clavecin*", when the composer was seven.

SONATES
POUR LE CLAVECIN
Qui peuvent se jouer avec l'Accompagnement de Violon
DEDIÉES
A MADAME VICTOIRE
DE FRANCE
Par J. G. Wolfgang Mozart de Salzbourg
Agé de Sept ans.
ŒUVRE PREMIERE
Prix 4.# 4 s
Gravées par Mme Vendôme Ci-devant rue St Jacques
à present rue St Honoré Vis-à-vis le Palais Royal
A PARIS 1767.
aux adresses ordinaires
AVEC PRIVILEGE DU ROI.
imprimé par petit blé

ABOUT THE WORKS IN THIS COLLECTION

Mozart's earliest clavier works were written in his sister's music book, the *Notebook for Nannerl.* His earliest known compositions, the *Andante* and *Allegro* K. 1a and b were written, his father Leopold noted, early in 1761, when he was five. They are very brief, and modeled on the little pieces, many of them north German in origin, that his sister had been given to play. A few other small pieces were composed between 1761 and 1763 (K. 2, 5b, and 6). During the winter months of 1764–65, while in London, Mozart started filling up a "London Notebook" with numerous small pieces. Many passages in these pieces reflect his acquaintance with music by his father, by numerous forgotten musicians, by fashionable German musicians who had settled in Paris, especially Schobert, Eckerd, and Honauer, by Wagenseil and Vanhal of Vienna, and by Rutini. Mozart seems to have tried writing for every form of instrumental music he knew.

These early works also show the influence of Johann Christian Bach, the youngest son of J. S. Bach, who lived in London at this time. Mozart expressed a "warmth and high esteem" for J. C. Bach throughout his life. They improvised together on the harpsichord, but it appears that Bach did not give Mozart lessons. All of the works indicated by the "K" number 15a, b, c, etc. date from this time in London. A few pieces contain the exact dates they were composed, notated by father Leopold.

ANDANTE IN B FLAT MAJOR, K. 5b (9b) *Page 22*

This unfinished piece was composed in the summer of 1763 and is outstanding. Here is Mozart's earliest example of passionate melancholy which later became so intensely personal to him. The whole piece is remarkable for the fluent power and certainty of its modulation and progressions, but specifically fine is the section between bars 19 and 34. Here we see the first budding of the plant which blooms to such poignant perfection in the masterly B minor *Adagio* (K. 540) of 1788. In this little *Andante* Mozart creates something which throws us off our rational balance, and by its striking originality makes direct appeal to our intuitive perception. Even though the unfinished piece ends in F major, by adding a *poco rallentando* in measures 35-36, it will effectively be brought to a close.

SICILIANO IN D MINOR, K. 15u *Page 28*

Notable in this piece is Mozart's association of the key of D minor with the rare siciliano rhythm, thus anticipating their union in the finale of the String Quartet K. 421 and in the last variation of the Violin Sonata in F major (K. 377).

ANDANTE IN G MINOR, K. 15r *Page 32*

The *Andante in G Minor* is a miniature sonata movement that is most attractive and full of confidence. G minor is one of Mozart's most evocative keys, and this little piece is tinged with some of his later fire and passion.

FANTASY IN D MINOR, K. 397 (385g) *Page 40*

The *Fantasy in D Minor* dates from either early 1782 or possibly from 1786-7. It is perfectly formed in three linked movements. After the opening modulating arpeggios suggesting Mozart's style when he improvised, this shortest of his fantasies soon turns lyrical in a passionate and melancholy *Adagio* section; it then finishes with a severe *allegretto* so short that we imagine the whole piece to be a splendid original prelude to more symmetrical movements. Mozart left the work unfinished, and the last ten bars, beginning at measure 87, were added by the editor of the Complete Edition published by Breitkopf and Härtel in 1804. This work appears to be influenced by Carl Philipp Emmanuel Bach and contains some romantic overtones.

RONDO IN D MAJOR, K. 485 *Page 45*

This *Allegro* movement is more strictly a sonata movement than rondo, for it has a full development and recapitulation. The ending is most interesting (from bar 136 to the end), where the main theme enters after a startling modulation from D major to B flat major, and then after a rhetorical flourish, adds an extra rhythmical tag, and with this expansion, dies away quietly and gracefully. The piece was written on January 10, 1786, for a female student. A dedication on the autograph has been erased, but some of it is still recognizable: "*Pour Mad*selle*: Charlotte de Wu. . .*" Perhaps the student in question was a Miss Würben or Würm, as both these names appear in a list of subscribers for Mozart's concerts in 1784. Mozart borrowed the theme of this Rondo from the Quintette, Opus 11, No. 6, of Johann Christian Bach.

Numerous contemporary reports suggest that Mozart tended to take his *allegro* movements at a moderate tempo. If Mozart wanted a movement to go very fast, he marked it *presto* or *allegro assai*. A plain *allegro* meant simply cheerful, or lively. This Rondo is highly effective when played cheerfully, graciously, or even in a flowing tempo. It is not nearly so interesting when played merely "fast"!

The grace notes before the quarters in bar one of the autograph are written like this:

They are to be performed like this:

TWELVE VARIATIONS ON "AH, VOUS DIRAI-JE, MAMAN," K. 300e (265) *Page 53*

This set of variations was composed in Paris in the early summer of 1778, where the tune was familiar and popular. In the United States this tune is known as "Twinkle, Twinkle, Little Star." The minor variation (No. VIII) has a pronounced intensity of feeling. These variations may have been composed for a student since there is much use of scales, arpeggios, and varying touches. It is one of Mozart's most charming sets, and is a rarity among his variations in that the autograph is extant, at least as a fragment.

Mozart's first composition, *Andante*, K. 1a, and a portion of the *Allegro*, K. 1b, written at five years of age. Marginal note is by Leopold Mozart.

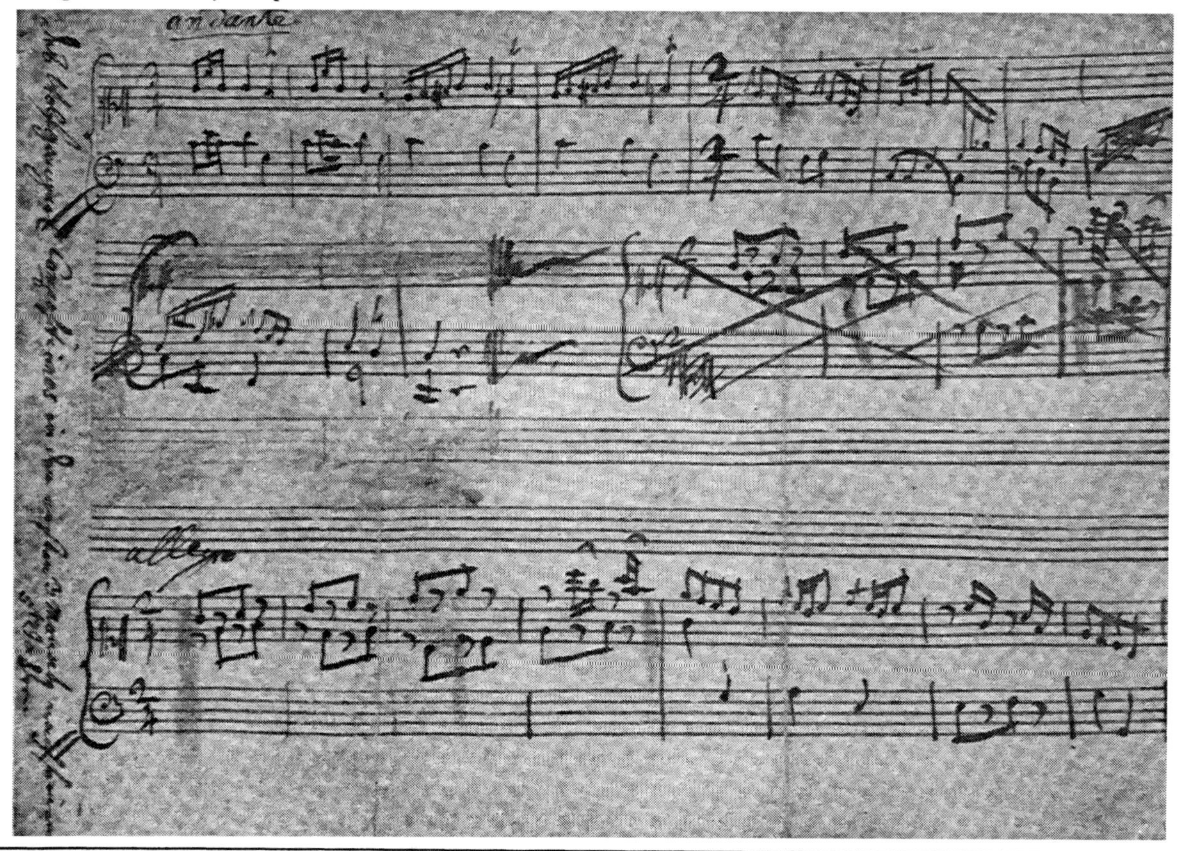

PERFORMING THE WORKS IN THIS COLLECTION

To perform Mozart's keyboard works in a stylistically correct manner, the pianist needs:

1. A smooth-flowing, clear and sparkling light touch. Light touch is especially important on our modern pianos because they have a tone that is almost too full for Mozart's music.
2. A tone quality that is refined and *cantabile* (singing) in melodic passages.
3. A physical approach that is devoid of unnecessary movement and affectation—mainly finger and hand technique. Mozart inherited a basic non-legato style of playing from the harpsichord era. He does often demand a legato (with the appropriate slurs) for melodic passages, but his accompanying figurations should almost always be played non-legato. Extended passages of triplets and sixteenths should be played non-legato. In Mozart's day most passages were *not* played legato unless specifically marked. Legato playing was the exception rather than the rule.

   Written: **Played:**

4. Interpretation concepts that should always be in the best of taste, with moderation in tempo, rubato and dynamics, and elegant phrasing.

TECHNICAL REQUIREMENTS

1. **Finger Action:**
   a. **Non-legato touch.** Keep the fingers as curved as possible for a tingly non-legato touch. Distinct finger action is required.
   b. **Legato touch.** Keep the fingers flatter, stretched out.
   Finger pressure is required. "Tie" the notes.

   Written: **Played:**

2. **Scales and arpeggios:** to play these even and without bumps, wrist must be elastic, and fast reactions in passing the thumb under are essential. Avoid the weak fourth and fifth fingers whenever possible. Thumb and fifth fingers may be used on black keys.
3. **Trills:** Trills should be even. For trills in these pieces try the following fingering: 1/3, 2/4, 3/5, 1/2, 2/3. Use the whole hand to shake, rotating from the elbow, plus the required finger movements.
4. **Octaves:** Broken octaves are frequent in Mozart (See *Klavierstück in F Major*, pg. 38; bars 1–10, 13–24). Rotate these octaves from the elbow. Keep the fingers in a fixed position.

PEDALING

The damper pedal should be used very sparingly with the pieces in this collection. Mozart left no pedal indications, yet he was enthusiastic about the knee-pedal mechanism on the Stein fortepiano. In a letter to his father dated October 17, 1777, he wrote:

> The device which you work with your knee is better than what is found on other instruments. You only need to touch it and it works, and as soon as you move your knee the least bit, you do not hear the slightest remainder of sound.

Mozart probably made limited use of the damper-pedal mechanism of his day. But in playing Mozart on the modern piano, pedal usage must be imperceptible, which will require very exact and frequent changes of pedal. Some of the fuller sounding arpeggios (i.e., the opening of the *Fantasy in D minor*) or chords may be held over with the fingers, often as long as the harmony doesn't change, this being the original meaning of playing *legatissimo*. Articulation, clarity of texture and phrasing should never be obscured.

The *una corda* (soft, or left) pedal should only be used when a definite alteration of tone quality is desired. Use of this pedal generally does not make the sound quieter, but alters its timbre.

All pedal indications in this collection are editorial and are only suggestions.

ORNAMENTATION

Mozart's ornamentation was always distinguished, tasteful, and mostly notated clearly. But some of his embellisments are ambiguous, and for that reason ornaments are realized in this collection either in the body of the score or by footnotes. Three rules generally consistent with the practices of Mozart's day are:

1. Ornaments are played on the beat.
2. Trills begin on the upper note (the pitch above the written note).
3. Mozart's trills are usually written to end with a turn. It is highly advisable to play the turn, even when it is not written.

To perform all the ornaments Mozart indicated is difficult even on old instruments (fortepianos). There will be passages for which the pianist should remember the old maxim that it is better to play a piece well without embellishments than to play it badly with them. Each situation must be determined by the artistic conscience of the pianist.

The best sources for information on Mozart's ornamentation are:

1. C. P. E. Bach. *Essay on the True Art of Playing Keyboard Instruments* (1753, 1762).
2. Leopold Mozart. *A Treatise on the Fundamental Principle of Violin Playing* (1756).
3. Daniel Gottlieb Türk. *School of Clavier Playing* (1789).

VARIED REPEATS

In Mozart's day it was customary for the performer to vary repeats. Mozart probably never played any of his repeated sections the same way. In the foreword to his *Sonatas with Varied Repeats* (1760), C. P. E. Bach wrote: "Today varied repeats are indispensable, being expected of every performer." Türk gives the following suggestions for varying repeats.

EIGHT BASIC RULES TO BE FOLLOWED BY PERFORMERS WHEN VARYING REPEATS
from Daniel Gottlieb Türk's *School of Clavier Playing* (1789)

1. Ornaments must fit the piece; players are not allowed to show off.
2. Arbitrary embellishments must be as good as what is written. This means that it may often be best not to vary.
3. The same types of ornaments should not be used too often. Extensive additions should be left for the end of the piece.
4. Additions must appear easy.
5. Pieces expressing sadness, seriousness, simplicity, pride, majesty or solemnity should not be varied.
6. Tempo must be strictly observed.
7. Each variation must be based on written harmony.
8. The bass may be varied in keyboard music, but the harmony must stay the same.

Türk further recommends that performers examine vocal treatises, such as those of Tosi and Hiller, who both encourage elaborate improvisation, since the same ornaments in vocal music usually work well on the keyboard.

From later treatises, such as Johann Peter Milchmeyer's *Die Wahre Art das Pianoforte zu Spielen* (1797) and A. E. Müller's *Fortepiano-Schule* (1825), it is clear that the practice of improvised ornamentation, and particularly varied repeats, continued throughout Mozart's lifetime and into the early nineteenth century, including early Beethoven.

ARTICULATION AND PHRASING

Articulation. Articulation means the style of delivery that is necessary to make clear the meaning of the musical text, including the smallest detail.

Phrasing. When we use the term "phrasing,"we mean a melodic section, such as a motive or theme, which is usually self-contained and which holds together as a musical whole.

Slurs. On the whole, Mozart's notation is rather complete, written out in great detail, and always with the most important interpretative element, the slurs. Even in movements which have hardly any dynamic marks in them, the slurs are always notated very carefully. Careful observance of the slurs is probably the single most important element in the proper interpretation of Mozart's music; connecting two notes which are separated by Mozart with either the finger or the pedal is the worst and most serious common fault in much Mozart playing.

Mozart used slurs to indicate: 1. *Legato.* A *legato* passage several bars long uses slurs that stop at the bar line, although in performance, no break between the bars is intended. 2. **Articulation.** There are short slurs over two, three, or sometimes four notes, and the final note is usually shortened.

Staccato Dots, Strokes and Wedge-Shaped Dashes. Mozart used the dot, the stroke, and the wedge-shaped dash to indicate staccato. But since a quickly written dot and/or wedge-shaped dash can degenerate into a short stroke, it is often difficult to tell which was intended. For this reason, I have used only the dot to indicate staccato in this edition. The comma (**,**) is used to assist the performer by defining the ends of phrases and/or articulated groups of notes.

Dynamics. Mozart used all the dynamic gradations between ***pp*** and ***ff*** (***pp***, ***p***, ***mp***, ***mf***, ***f***, ***ff***), crescendo and diminuendo, but his use of ***p*** and ***f*** were used as merely basic types. The marking ***p*** can mean ***p***, ***mp***, or ***pp***, while ***f*** can mean ***mf*** to ***ff***. The pianist must decide in each case which level is to be used. The editor has added dynamic suggestions where Mozart did not leave any.

THE PURPOSE OF THIS EDITION

Unfinished oil painting by Mozart's brother-in-law, Joseph Lange. (*Mozart Museum, Salzburg.*)

The purpose of **At the Piano with Mozart** is to present a varied collection of some of Mozart's finest keyboard music, and to assist the pianist and the piano teacher in interpreting this magnificent music, based on performance practices in Mozart's time. Attention has been focused for the most part in this collection on just exactly what it is Mozart expects the performer to do with his score. It is impossible to know exactly how this music was performed during Mozart's era because we cannot reproduce the scents and sounds of the past, and we do know that performance practices change. As the Earl of Rochester noted long ago, "*Since 'tis Nature's Law to change, Constancy alone is strange.*" This volume came into being with the hope that it would help the pianist to be faithful to Mozart's works of art, which after all is our principal aim in performance.

Most pianists using this collection will perform this music on a twentieth-century piano, even though it was originally written for harpsichord and fortepiano. Therefore, our suggestions on how to play this music in a more stylistically correct manner should be very helpful to the pianist and the piano teacher. All editorial marks and suggestions have been added with this fundamental concept in mind—how to most effectively play this music on our present-day pianos.

Historical information surrounding the compositions and information from Mozart's own letters have been included to help clarify his style of performance. This correspondence is an indispensable documentary source for reconstructing the interpretive style of the period. All dynamic, pedal, and metronome marks are editorial, except where indicated otherwise. Fingering is also editorial and should help the performer to realize clearly the articulation recommended in each piece. First and early editions as well as some autographs have been consulted. The pieces are arranged progressively according to difficulty, thereby allowing the student a clearer understanding of Mozart's style—from early and more simple, to later and more mature.

The "K" numbers refer to Köchel's *Chronologisch-thematisches Verzeichnis sämtlichen Tonwerke W. A. Mozarts* (Chronological, Thematic List of the Complete Works of W. A. Mozart). The first edition of this list was compiled by Ludwig von Köchel, and published in 1862. Subsequent revised versions (1937, 1947, and 1965) contained supplementary numbers and revisions. Where there are two numbers assigned, the latest appears in parentheses.

I am grateful to the Library of Congress for assistance in locating the unfinished *Andante in B flat Major*, K. 5b (9b).

Maurice Hinson

Minuet in F Major

Tempo di menuetto (♩ = 126)

K. 2

Composed in Salzburg in January 1762. Mozart's minuets must have three clear beats in a bar, not one.

Allegro in C Major

K. 1b

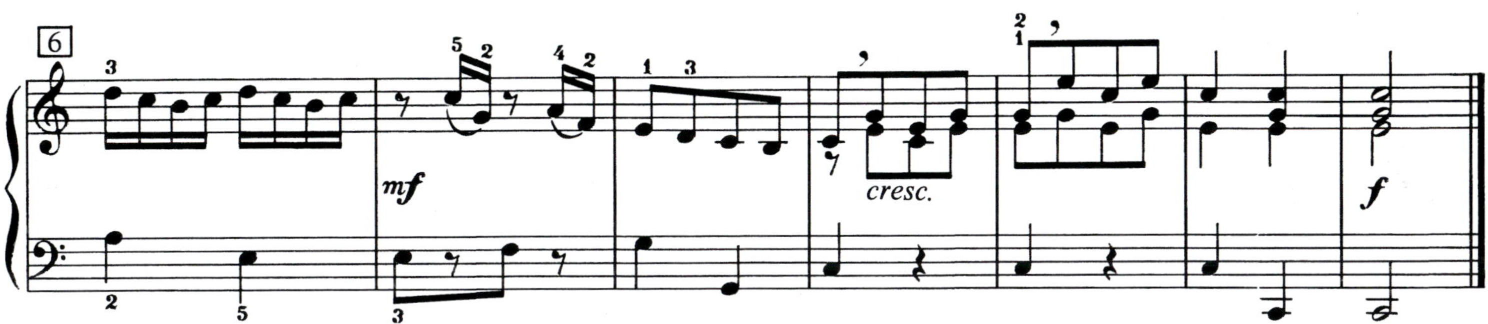

Allegro is Mozart's most common tempo marking and covers everything that comes under the heading "quick".

Andante in C Major

K. 1a

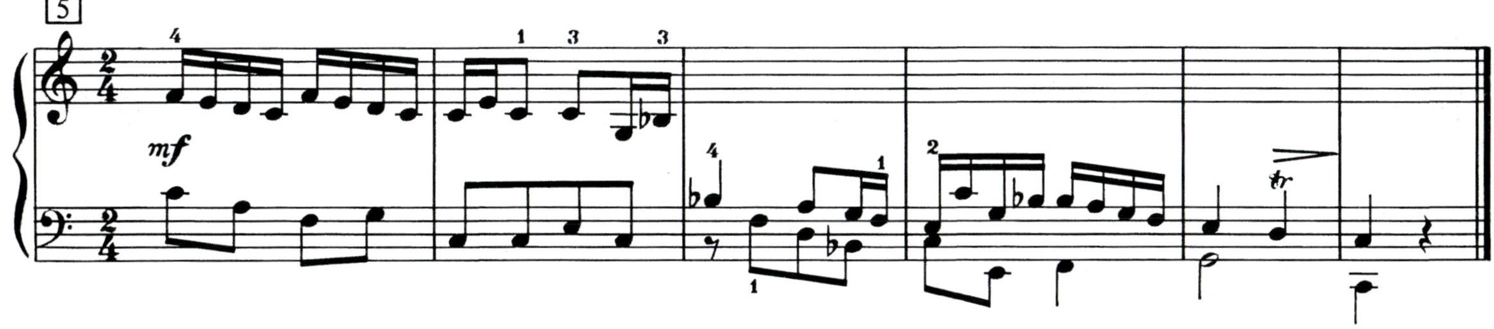

This piece was composed by Wolfgang in the third month of his fifth year.

Minuet II in F Major

Composed by Wolfgang on July 16, 1762.

Allegro in B-flat Major

K. 3

Composed in Salzburg on March 4, 1762.

Andante in B-flat Major

K. 5b (9b)

See page 12 for discussion of this piece.

ⓐ The autograph contains a "B♭" here, but it appears to be an obvious error.

19
p
f
23
p
f
27
31
35
mf
poco rit.
mp

Minuet in D Major

K. 315a (315g)

Andante con moto (♩ = 132)

TRIO

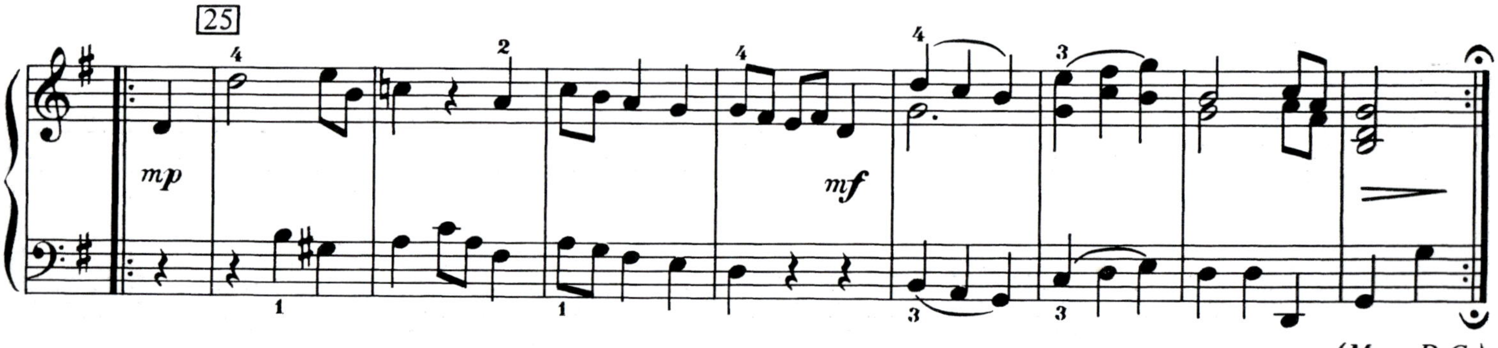

(Men. D.C.)

Pieces from "The London Notebook"

Composed in 1764-65

Allegro in F Major

K. 15a

Minuet in G Major

K. 15c

Moderato (♩ = 126)

5

9

13

17

Rondino in D Major

K. 15d

Siciliano in D Minor

The *Siciliano* is a fairly slow piece in compound duple meter, with dotted rhythm, similar to the *Pastorale.* The genre derived from a Sicilian dance type and was cultivated primarily during the seventeenth and eighteenth centuries.

Country Dance in G Major

Allegro (♩ = 104)

K. 15e

f

6

mf

11

p

mf

f

Andante in A Minor

K. 15k

Gracefully (♩ = 108)

Country Dance in A Major

ⓐ The half-trill (pralltriller) works well at this tempo.

Andante in G Minor

K. 15r

43
mf
49
mp
mf
55
f
61
mf
68
mp
p
pp

Rondo in F Major

K. 15hh

Allegretto to Mozart is much like *Andante* and only moderately fast.

32
p
40
47
mp
cresc.
53
mp
58
cresc.
D.C.

March in F Major

K. 8

Allegro maestoso (♩ = ca. 72)

Composed by W.A. Mozart in Paris on November 21, 1763. *Allegro maestoso* is slightly slower than *Allegro*. Leopold Mozart characterized it as majestic, deliberate, not rushed. Both Quantz and Türk advocate use of echo dynamics in their treatises, as seen in this piece.

29
34
39
44
49
poco rit.

Klavierstück in F Major

(Piano Piece)

ⓐ This piece is not included in the Köchel list. Mozart composed it during the end of August and the beginning of September 1766.

Andantino in E-flat Major

K. 236 (588b)

This *Andantino* is rather like a flowing *Andante* merged with the character of the minuet.

Fantasy in D Minor

ⓐ The omission of this tie in the original edition was probably an engraver's error.

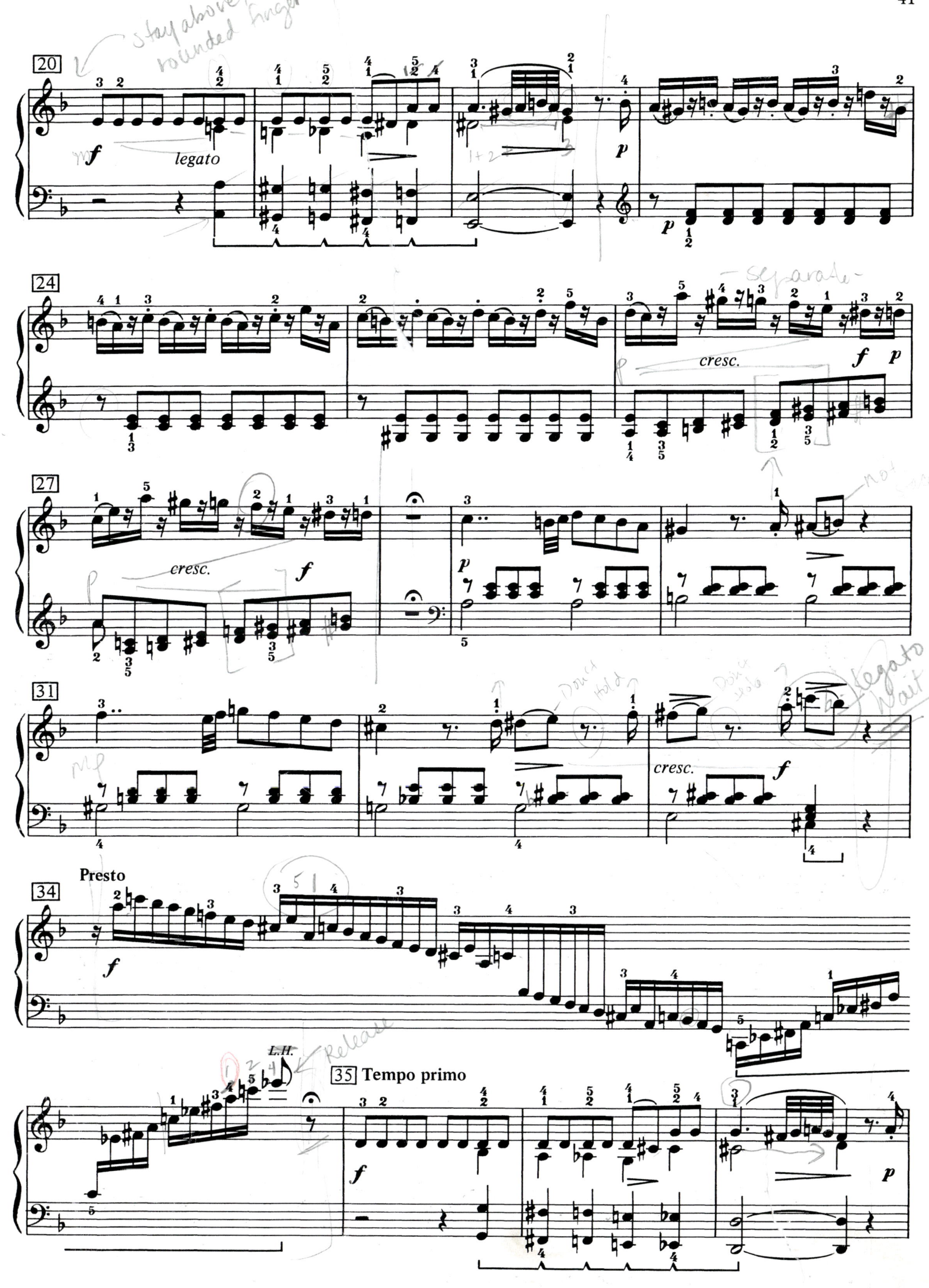
20
legato
24
cresc.
27
cresc.
31
cresc.
34
Presto
L.H.
35 Tempo primo

38
41
cresc.
f p
cresc.
f
Presto
44
mf
dim.
mp
p
poco rit.
45
Tempo primo
p
49
f
p
fp

53
cresc.
55
Allegretto (♩ = 120)
dolce
63
69
1.
2.
73

78
83
87
a tempo
rall.
93
101

Rondo in D Major

Composed in Vienna on January 10, 1786.

19
23
28
32
36
cresc.
p
mf
mp

40
44
47
51
55
60
p
mf
cresc.
f
p
f

66
p
cresc.
f
dim.
70
mf
74
78
cresc.
82
f

86
89
93
poco rit.
mf
97
101
p
pp
104
f

109
112
mf
116
120
123
pp
mf

126
129
132
135
tr
mp
139
f
143

146
mf
149
153
p
157
cresc.
p
cresc.
162
p
calando
pp
a
b Calando means getting quieter and slower.

Twelve Variations on "Ah, vous dirai-je, Maman"

K. 300e (265)

ⓐ We suggest ***pp*** non legato in the repeats.

ⓑ The autograph contains trills in the right hand on the first count of measures 49, 59, 63, and on the second count of measure 65.

57

pp

61

p

cresc.

65

mf

69

73 **Var. III**

ⓒ

f

77

repeat p

ⓒ Play each trill as a half-trill (pralltriller) since there is not enough time to play a full trill.

81
pp
85
p
89
mp
93
97
Var. IV
f
101
repeat p

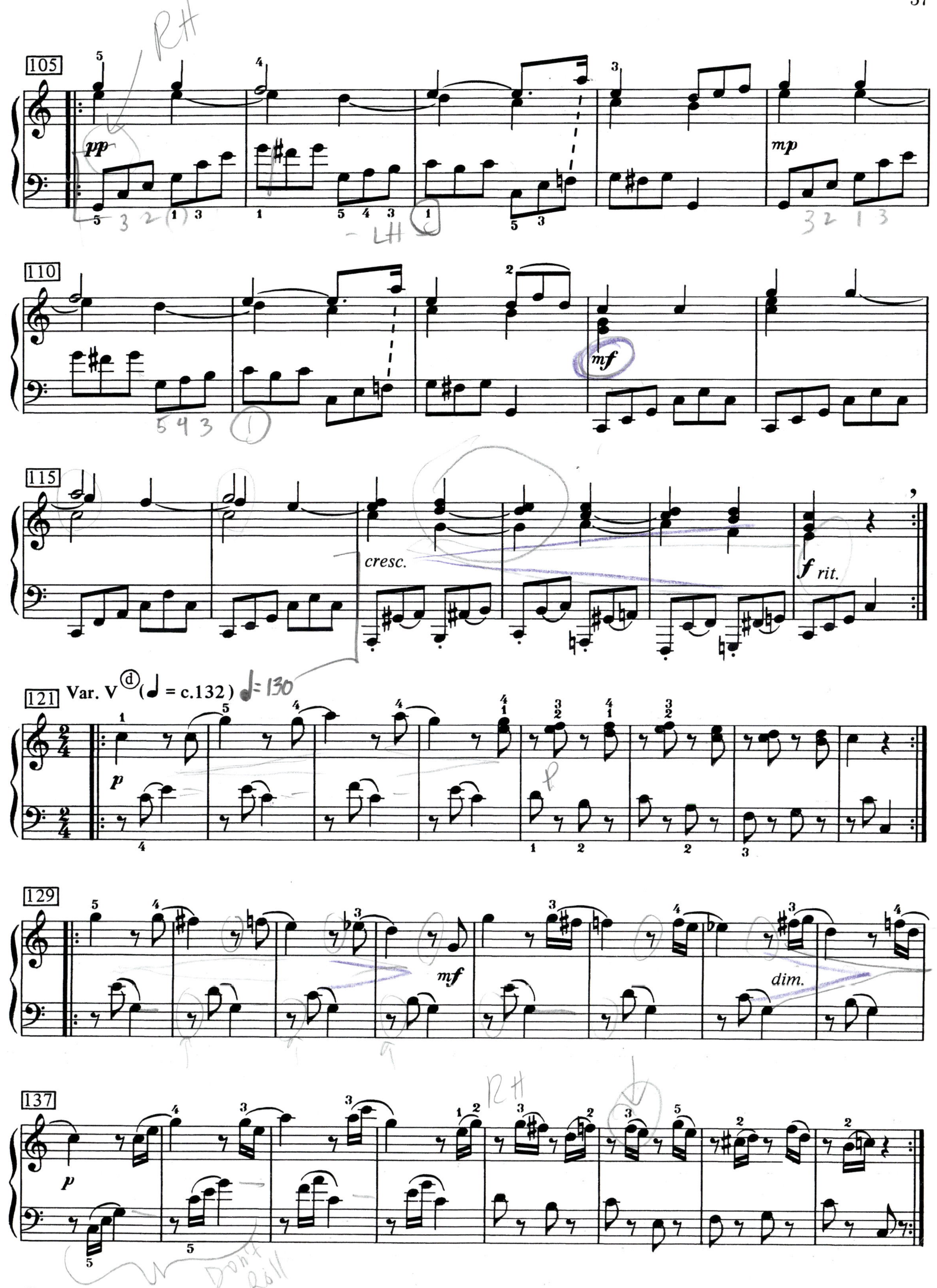

ⓓ Play this variation with great delicacy and very lightly.

ⓔ Play the sixteenths, especially those in the left hand, clearly and non legato.

ⓕ Should be played with sparkling virtuosity.

(g) Simple, *cantibile* style, *legato* throughout except for the original *staccato* dots at m. 208 and 209.

ⓗ Perform with virtuosity.

ⓘ Very expressive and with flexible dynamics.

ⓙ High spirited, clear, with virtuosity, but do not produce a powerful sound.

306
309
312
314
317
320
Cresc
Lift
Lift
rit.
Hold
f